The Other Side Of Me

A book of love poems

By

Gart Paulson DeShong

Dedication

I give thanks to my God and Lord for all the gifts He has embedded in me, which I share with the world. I pray that hearts will be blessed and filled with joy, and that my words will not only be mere words, but words full of life, meaning, and light for the soul. This book is also dedicated to Lyrics & Intro.

Acknowledgement

A special thank you to my coworkers, Shevy Miller, Roxanne Ralph, Romano Ince, and Josiah Thomas.

A special thank you to my mom, Yvette Brown.

A special thank you to my dearest aunties, Irene and Marcell Deshong.

A special thank you to Donna "Teeri" Hazelwood.

A special thank you to Anica Jack.

A special thank you to my two angels, Radia "Lyrics" Deshong and Ronia "Intro" Dehsong.

A special thank you to Andrew Clarke and Dr. Orando Brewster.

A special thank you to Abina White.

A special thank you to Jonte Myers, Greg Myers, Adia Douglas, and Falana Myers. I love you all beyond words.

A special thank you to Ranan Jerry.

THE OTHER SIDE OF ME

Arrested

I'm so locked up in love
Don't want to be free
Love this feeling; nothing can be better than this
With heart and soul can't resist

You made me so happy
Totally, totally, completely happy
This love is so different
Feel fresh like a sweet fragrance

I'm feeling you that deep
Have no choice but to accept defeat
Got me falling from my place
Into your warm embrace

So fast my heart melt down
Instant connection emotions come down
This is a special moment
That I cannot comment

It all started with the eye contact
Nothing I can do to stop that
You're downloaded in my spirit
Between us, there is so much magic

29-6-2022

Please Don't Do It To Me

Please don't do it to me
Baby don't close the door on me
I'm begging with all of me
With the rest of what's left inside of me
Please have some sympathy with me
I know I ain't been perfect
In the closet, I have so many secrets
I'm really trying to be honest with you.
To do so, God knows, is the hardest thing to do
Even though so many times I lied to you.
Baby! Baby! I really love you
Believe we can still make it
Doing the right thing, I will practice
When I don't see or hear from you for a day
Like getting up without saying a prayer
My spirit becomes so weak
The joy of missing you is incomplete
What I've done is not something I'm proud of
Oh! Lord, I need the grace of your love
This is a new experience for me
Living a life without you
Going through what I'm going through
I wish of being true to you
As I open my eyes
My mistakes I see make my pressure rise
Even though we're finished I can't give up
Losing you is way too much

20-10-2022

Oh Sugar

Sitting up in my room at this time
Of the night with you on my mind
Put me in the right mood
Got me feeling all good
With the picture of you in my head
Like a sweet dream can't get out of my head
You don't know how I feel
From my heart feelings began to reveal
Wanna stay forever don't want to leave
You took me by the sleeves
Thoughts of you stay with me
Like energy keeps me going daily
You're the perfect gift I could ever find
With you, I will never change my mind
Every time I really wanna see you
I'm lightened with the sweetness of you
This is so so awesome
It will take time to overcome
I'm taken by your beauty and charisma
You're the best and will be the best ever
Your incomparable beauty and grace
The radiance of it lightened up my face
You will never go out of style
You'll never go out of style even if days, or months and
years go by.

12-11-2022

Wonderful Beauty

When I look at your awesome beauty
It's such a great joy to see
you are amazing my love
you are amazing my love so so amazing my
so so amazing my love
God does something extra special for you
I see the expression of his handy work on him
so excellent like glory above the heavens
So excellent like glory above the heavens
the effect you have on me has no one
I'm consumed by your infinite beauty
With gladness and adoration, I looked at you continuously
The feeling I got is really indescribable
Like melodies from up above unexplainable
Beauty blesses me more and more every day
it gives me a feeling that never gonna fade away
Oh yes! I love it, I love it, truly love it
I'm so touched, nothing could ever be that perfect
So majestic you are in all my thoughts
you are a blessing to my heart
makes me fall in love with you every time
it gets me better than the first time.

19-6-2022

Got Me Over

The moment I saw you, got me saying oh oh
Smooth and rich like my favorite cookie Oreo
Taken me like a sweet temptation
Cannot describe my reaction
I had to take a deeper breath
Put my hands to my chest heartbeat to death
Got me falling so hard over you
Won't take a chance gambling with you
Cause I know I'm gonna lose to you
The feelings I'm getting tell me it's true
You are first on my wish list
Never experienced nothing like this
You're fabulous damn, you break me
As my heart gives way to you completely
The way you touch me I can't think
Like a man can't hold his drink
You give me feelings that leave scars on me
Like the sun set on me so beautifully
Hard for me to put it in context
Because this is so iconic
Broke me down to the flesh and bone
Still can't leave you alone.

6-08-2022

Not Your Portion

Your status is not a side chick
You don't deserve it
I can see you deep in thoughts
something on your mind
and it's troubling the heart
bothering you all the time
you deserve your own lover
gave you roses candy and flower
you need to be loved and kissed
share your life with that one call you Mrs.
You don't need to be on standby
Waiting on a call from the guy
when the rain is falling you all alone
while he is in the warm embrace at home
hard for you to function in the right mind
that arms to hold you so short you can't find
the situation is driving you crazy
because you calling him and he is with his baby
even though she is getting the best of you
still, it's hard for me to be faithful but I do
know that you can come home to me every day
this is all my fault anyway
if I'm not the only one
don't wanna be in any competition
my temperature drops when it's cold
there's no fire to warm the soul
this relationship gives me nothing but frustration
how you want me to really understand
tired of all this hide and seek
feels like a slap on the cheek
feelings come and go constantly
hard for us to grow believe me
many times, I take the bottle for my Companion

take one, two, three drinks, do it hard and strong
put nothing in it to break it down
I go to bed when I get drunk
let us leave each other on good terms
so that there will be no bad storm
this can't work for me no more
need someone for me that I could love and adore.

29-6-2022

Mamma, You're My Hero

you're the backbone of the family
the cornerstone of the family
I can't lose with you in my life
I love you so much like the role you played in my life
I've grown on you in a good way
My super mother taught me how to pray

Mothers like you don't born no more
so proud you are my mama, loved you for evermore
you are a mother to be praised
I like the way I was raised
Your love is made of pure gold
priceless it shines in my soul
your love and teaching have your signature on it
you nursed me from my hurt and pain
And you give me my name

A very important part in my life you played
Cause I wouldn't be the person that I am today
I put my trust in your trust
All the time you never wrong that's a plus
You always have my back
Even if I'm wrong you tell me how it is, no matter what
You're the best that there ever was
You filled my life with the joy of your love
Thank you for your discipline and counsel
Forever and ever you are my hero.

14-1-2023

Absolutely Gorgeous

Your beauty can never be beaten
You are the condensed milk that's sweetened
like you drop out of heaven
you are blessed amongst all women
every time I see you I see perfection
full me up with total satisfaction
Never get tired of admiring you
nothing can get any better than you
oh I love to see your eyes
They speak to me "The come here eyes"
Like to see you're going out and you're coming in
The way you walk is a marvelous thing hypnotizing
You are like daddy's little girl
The one he always spoiled
Who he loved out of the world
Can't say nothing more that hasn't been said
Got me saying yes while shaking my head
You grace my heart like an Angel
The way you look has no rival
None at all, whatsoever
You draw attention from all sorts of nature
You are so so glorious
A shining star, you're so precious
You are spectacular from head to toe
I will stand up all night to see you tomorrow
It's impossible not to want Someone Like You
If it has a face, it would be you
you make me wonder in my mind
My eyes follow you, like a camera, taking pictures of you
every time

17-11-2022

Standard

Eyes and eyes have seen you
Kind of girl makes me wanna love you,
Cause me to say oh oh oh oh
Hell hell hell hell hello
I will turn water into wine
For you, I will make time
Trying to get my heart calm down
Keeps racing, hard to cool down
You are my standard
get me walking backwards
I'm shouting out glory Hallelujah
take my hands and make the prayer sign
you deserve all the applause
baby, forever I wanna be yours
impose myself on you gracefully
caught up in your amazing beauty
Never will do you wrong to say I'm so sorry
for in every way you are worthy, worthy
I'm impressed by you across the board
my praises of you are beyond words
never been so astonished before
can't get enough of you for sure
I wasn't expecting this at all
Without hesitation, I took the fall
my baby, my baby please come yah
desire you to stay with me forever ah
I could love you forever

2-10-2022

I Could Love You Forever

First time I saw you I got nervous
I could not keep my focus
feelings started to pour into my heart
Butterflies took over my heart
you made me sweat in the middle of my hand
something I could never understand
your image cemented in my mind at this time
it struck me like the very first time
this heart begins to float on feelings
the more I look at you it gets deeper in my system
you took me all the way to the very end
Oh my! Oh my! This I can't comprehend
I'm willing to share my world and space with you
It's so easy to fall in love with you
just can't function in your presence
for sure I know I feel so different
this is not fear, fright nor anxiety
After all this time it still happens to me
From day unto day and night to night
it keeps growing and growing taking over my life
the kind of feeling that pours in my spirit
It's so good there is no limit
You give me more joy than in a rich harvest
see my life it's a true witness
it's so crazy when I look into your eyes
every time I do, I'm so mesmerized
with you, it's a continuous history
which makes sweet, sweet memories.

Influence

This is all crazy but worth it
the fact I can't get enough of it
neither can I say no
you got me so, cannot let you go
needs to take a hold of myself
nothing I do can ever help
you break me down every time
thoughts of you inhabit my mind
every memory of you weakens me
All of my emotions grow rapidly
like a bad habit taking advantage of me
the thing that it does really?
Lost my way like a blind man
Bound together we became as one
I've got to hold on for my sanity
There is no way simply for me to break free
It feels so empty without you
Don't have a clue how to live without you
This thing is stronger than the finest liquor
And smooth so good it takes me over
Am drunken twenty-four seven
I lost myself every time it happens
I'm craving, I'm consumed with it
steadfastly locked on, must commit
my candy bars, snickers baby milk payday
nuggle, butterfinger and milky way
You are so different in all dimensions
you fill me up with so much passion
I cannot shake you off
I cannot eat you off
my addiction of you is incurable
it reaches me on all levels
3-11-2022

No One But You

You've lighted my fire
nothing will quench this desire
You do a new thing in my life
Excites me both day and night
You are necessary to me
Every time I see you, you're like God's glory
can never lose sight of you
you are everything I hold fast to
I'll treat you good for you're my own
I'm enlightened by you greatly
You sat in my heart for eternity
Enjoy you like the fruit of my labor
You made me better and richer
will maintain my covenant with you
Like faith that takes me through
My life in you mean everything to me
I'm after you, like the Lord pursue me
I can never fail with you
Maintain a pure heart for you
You gave me sweet peace and content
Like a sacrifice that brings great results in the end
You are that seed that grows in every way
My blessing that manifests every day.

20-11-2022

Faithful Love

What I become is because of you
I'll never draw away from you
It's not for bread or what I can get from you
I'm here because I truly love you
You never ever failed me
I love you beyond the flesh
for your love has no season
the essence of it will never come to an end
water cannot quench my thirst for you
Nothing could ever take me away from you
Neither any riches of this world
No gold, silver, diamond or Pearl
You are priceless to me in every way
Uphold my life like a fervent prayer
You mean more to me than physical things
Can feel you in my life increasing
You've been good and continue to do good
And I see the good, getting better
It's shining brighter and brighter
I could never forget your goodness
Makes my soul so rich and bless
Gives me a smile and a wonderful feeling
Every day of my life it's showing
Nobody will remove you from out of my heart

The way that you are treating me
Is so good I experience it in my life continuously

18-12-2022

Delicately

Like to put my arms around you
With comfort of hugs, I embrace you
Arms stayed around you right through
Spirit of love doing it for me and you
As I look at you breathing
It's such a beautiful, beautiful thing
like to feel it up on my skin
Soothes my heart like the sound of violin
The breath out of nostril like cool breeze blowing
There is such peace and quietness all around
like staring at the snow coming down
Wow! There is no word for this
So enjoyable like a perfect kiss
Like the wind blowing gently through the trees of the field
Hearts are smiling endlessly can never be this real
the softest of touch like a baby holding your hand
just have to stop and give it more attention
the moment sinks in you, like the seawater into the sand
I gave my heart to you in the palm of your hand
So gently meek and mild like the woman that touched Jesus'
garment
never felt this good, the sweetest of moment
I hold you in my care
Forever you are in my prayer

2-10-2022

My Heart Is For You

You're all that I need to know
For all of my tomorrows
when this world comes to an end
and it starts all over again
it's still gonna be you yes you
heart can't stop beating for you
I see you with my eyes closed
when the light of your beauty glows
I am so dear to you
Like the sky and its blue
without you, nothing cannot work
for you are my favorite life support
Pour all of my love into your love
Your love lost minds equal infinity love
The times when I am most happy
Is when I am with you truly
All the goodness I receive is from your hands
So priceless to me means more than billions
I totally lack nothing with you
Long as my soul lives, I'll never leave you

14-6-2022

Virtuous One

You alone make me happy
love surrounding me like family
Treat you like sugar in my tea
Full to my taste completely
I can never go wrong with you
Don't wanna grow without you
Gives you everything you ever ask for
Know you will turn it into millions and more
You never disappoint me with your love
It's like new blessings coming blown from above
You, I will never ever underestimate
All that you've done for me, I appreciate
And will continue to do for you for years to come
A love like you I could never overcome
You are irreplaceable to me
More than all of the world's money
Every day I see things improving
My life never stopped growing
I reaped the rewards because of you
I feel so special loving you
Joy you give me it's unexplainable
Touch me through and through so incredible
Always lift me up when I'm down
your smile radiates my life like the sun
You correct me when I'm wrong
Always there to keep me strong
When you speak to me I listen
Don't wanna fix what's never been broken
You will forever remain relevant
For in every way you are important

16-7-2022

The Love Of My Life

Though I have made many mistakes
your love for me you never forsake
I may not be perfect
Desire for me, you'll never forfeit
Though I may stray so many times
In your arms a place I always find
When I was unkind to you
You never stop loving me no matter what I do
I felt cheated on you doing so, i'm guilty
You needed me more than I can see
When I took you for granted and ignored you
You overlooked it all with a loving heart
The action you take troubled my thoughts
The pleasures of this world didn't fulfil my desire
After a while, they could not satisfy my hunger
Eyes were open to see the way you love me
I could never be the person I used to be
To be in love with is more than anything that I value
Like the blessings of the morning view
It never stops, it keeps on falling through
You're worth it
You deserve it
I wouldn't' choose another to be my love forever
Many times I fall and wanna give up
You came and picked me up saying my grace is enough
I've failed you over and over again
You who began a good work in me is able to finish it to the
end
You are like no other
Your love is richer than all treasures
You never fake it with me
You keep it real with me
There is no competition with you

All I desire is intimacy with you
You never close no door on me
No gold nor riches can replace you
If I had to live my life over again
I will choose you first above all else over and over again

16-7-2022

So So Love You

You triggered me on various levels
touch me in a deeper place
you're a nonstop admiration
cause my heart to make excellent reaction
I'm stumbling for words
Like I'm taken up between the earth and heaven
First time I've never been that scared
heart is saying to me don't be afraid
You bring comfort and give me affection
Never felt this good all of my life
come explain moments like there
So real makes my heart freeze
There is no space in my brain
for no one else but you
You fulfill my life like words of a prophecy
Your love goes in hard on me
I feel value with you that I can see
You level me up completely
Now I can see things clearly
Not seeing any more tree
Your caring is what I was missing
I'm so glad the essence of it is captivating
The kind of things you brought to the table
Confidence wisdom, strength, keeps me stable
Everything that you do is right on point
The right person that I always needed
No one can ever be better than you
Don't have to look back on what I went through
You're all the pieces that make me up
I'm so fortunate to have you in my life
My love for you is unconditionally
You saved my life and fix it thoroughly
you made my life a classic

Lives on for years and years to come
You are my breakthrough blessing
Surpassed my expectation and everything
with you, there's are no rules or regulation
You and I are an awesome combination
I have to up and tell you
nothing! Absolutely nothing can match you
Girl you not my wanty wanty
But you are my needy needy
No love like you

20-7-2022

It's All Over Now

Hold your tears please don't cry
They can't mount up to all of your lies
No more feeling sorry for you
I know all the things that you do
now you see the other side of me
there is no more mercy
Heart is not so soft any more
time for me to close the door
You can never call me like before
All of your sweet words I'm gonna ignore
Time enough for me to be me
can't deal with your weak ass apology
Your luck has finally run out
Didn't know I would have figured it out
Time has a way of showing you it
Every secret that lies in the closet
No more eating by your worries and stress
And being consumed with pain and unhappiness
The hard way of learnt my lesson
Everything happens for a reason
You can fix a broken eggshell
I know how to get out of hell
I gave you love, peace and forgiveness
that's the way I send you off to the world of darkness
Got to let you go bye bye
wish I had never known you that's no lie
I can go out again
Enjoy myself with my friends
Regaining all my life, strength and energy
Not going to take no shit from anybody

23-9-2022

Baby! Baby! I'm Missing You

Standing here in a wishing mood
The way I feel inside is not good
Loneliness makes my life fade away
My life is filled with cold nights and days
Like the ocean without the water
So is my tea without the sugar
There is no sweetness in my life
For I took the wrong advice
Need one more chance to be with you
My coldest times are without you
Cannot deal with the absence of you
God knows I don't know what to do
No! No! I cannot live like this
Missed your touch, hugs, smile and kiss
Consumed by my stupid mistakes
No more gifts, blowing out of candles on birthday cake
I didn't care about your feelings
When I was enjoying my dealings
Every day I'm praying for a super miracle
Not giving up that's not where I'm gonna settle
Please don't be mad at me forever
Don't want you to be another man's treasure
Oh, baby! I Repent of my wrong doing
Not going to do my own thing again
Never say that word to me, it's over, move on
No way I can deal with it heart is not strong
There are no more happy days

All I have is dark and silent days
Don't hold me of the past I've seen what it has done to me
I've paid the prize a million times already
grief added to my sorrow
Right now my vision is dark can't see tomorrow
I have no rest, fainted in my sighing
For my eyes are swollen because of crying
I'm gonna be living on my knees
Until you accept my apology.

26-9-2022

Something More Perfectly

I know my love that loves me
It's not of the ordinary
And it cares for me unconditionally
I feel you beyond all intimacy
Experienced love that's like no other
Keeps getting better as we grow together
Love you more than a million love
For you give me the truest of love.
Have fellowship with you daily
You become so important to me
The spirit shines forth as brightness
My life fill with joy and happiness
The deepest part of me I give to you
I'm dead to all others but not you
You are precious to the core
I could not love anyone more
My heart is satisfied with you
Nothing is too hard to give you
Because you took me as nothing
And turned me into something
I will never give up on you no way
Partner with you for the price you pay
You become my life, invested everything in you
It is so incredible with you, don't even have a trust issue
Trade everything for you
For I see your true value
I put no there before you

3-12-2022

Star In My Heart

Turn my eyes to see your face
Hold my chest as my heart began to race
Halt at the position of attention
Took a deep breath as I tried to stand
Looking at you from all directions
I could not hold my position
You are a good one to keep
For you make life fully complete
Don't have to wonder no more
You are all that I desire forever more
I know the sweetest life, will be with you
Living together in a world of me and you
No one will ever be better
Need you to be my love forever
You would not fail like God's mercies
You're blessed with all the right qualities
I will fight for you so true
That and more I will do
You are someone I need now
Still need you a thousand years from now

23-10-2022

Attractive

Like a flower shows forth its blossom
The beauty of it I can't ignore
Draws me closer, picture is so awesome
So sweet my heart adores
Fell in love just looking at you
For all the time I wanna admire you
You take roots in me, like a tree by the water
Get so much life that it will not wither
I'm connected to you spiritually and physically
A natural attraction that I always wanted to see
Feelings I get from looking at you are unexplainable
Sparks a fire in me, I become so vulnerable
It's truly a beautiful, beautiful feeling
Felt it in my soul the impact is so genuine
wanna associate myself with you
The more and more I look at you
your beauty goes straight to the soul
This is so good, more expensive than gold
You crush me 1000 times and still counting
It surpasses all my knowledge and understanding
There is no one more beautiful than you on the earth
The proof is there, the way you took my heart
The way you look, your features are killing me
You destroy every part of me most definitely
In a good way, you're a problem to me
And I can't get rid of you, for you amazes me sincerely
Your infectious beauty takes hold of me, cause me to watch
you over and over
The effect you have on me, I'm struggling to recover
You embodied me, strikes me like nature
echoed in me like the song of many waters bye

4-6-2022

I Was Made For You

I'll never exchange your love, to me it's everything
My will is to love you for my living
Life I'm living is on a different level
Never felt this cool it's all incredible
You made my life a million times better
It shines out like the beauty of a flower
You are the one that brings me, abundant love
I know you are my most precious prize
you perfectly fit in my profile
Joy takes my soul, can't stop smile
I'm taken by the feelings of sweet happiness
You fill out the blank spaces in me, you're the best
Life is rest from sadness and at peace
can't explain the way my life has increase
Taught me how to love in true essence
My soul mate, a love of great reference
Nothing will ever put out this light
it shines and brightens up my entire life
Takes care of me with your heart
I see you have a pure and clean heart
Make it easier for me to love you
Took away doubt and increase my trust in you
I'm not going back to the past
You gave me love that I'll never surpass

2-06-2022

Blooming flower

The light of your beauty
shines out so richly
The image of it captivating
it got me in deep thinking
The way you glow, I'm mesmerized
Don't wanna even wink my eyes
You are so beautiful and that is true
It goes from the heart of you
You will never lose your charm
because you got it in every form
You have an amazing face
The face of all faces
Capture the attention of human eyes even birds and bees
The image of your beauty, it magnificent to see
I looked at you and see heaven
Endless beauty without an end
richest flower I've ever seen, so incredible
There's none of your kind, you're irreplaceable
Such a radiance you give off as you grow
Pleasant to the sight, in the wind you glow
The one and only forever- blooming flower
Like a rainbow shines in many colors

20-6-2022

Hallow One

You! Are the only one
That I will ever love
I don't want to look back
For I have no reason to do that
All I ever need is in front of me
There's no partition between you and me
Because you truly love me
When I was blind to me
in you I've have found all my needs
the only love that I breathe
Can't lose you out of my life
Where you brought me from, need you forever in my life
You took me to a different place
I feel so much peace in this place
My life is growing in ways of you
The things I do is never to hurt you
you are my fire in the cold
Heat of your love warms my soul
You'll never sit in anyone's shadow
I'll hold on to you and will not let go
Silver and gold can't satisfy like you do
After a time they lost their value but you never do
You're the only good thing I've ever found
Forever and ever, I need you around
Every day I experience something new with you
Eternity is not enough to love you

14-12-2022

Extra Sweet

Feel so special with you
Morning from the old into the new
Never thought I could have felt this way
Everything changed since you came my way
it's such a total release for me
you're the point of difference to me
made me feel to love you by the things you do
for the rest of my life, that's what I'm going to do
my whole life you have aligned
can breathe freely because of Peace of Mind
you are the prize of my life
I became a person of great value
the best moment of my life is with you
I can't ignore all the things that you've done
and continue to do it so awesome
this is ironic beyond belief, make me marvel
the one that takes my life to another level
I'm blessed with the sweetest of love
I'm so happy with myself now
No one compares to your matchless love
I got back that joyful spirit now
I've gotten many wins that I'm very proud of
first time I'm well taken care of
Can't explain how happy and fulfilled I am
Seeing myself first place in everything and not second
Heart will not suffer, hurt and be sorrowful again
You brought all those things to an end

27-12-2022

Speak to me

I'm feeling so into it
Can't escape this chick
Don't know how you got me feeling like this
Thoughts of you I cannot resist
It seems to me like I got hit
Down the lane, I need another trip
Like the feeling that you bring
Damn! You are so soothing
You got me all up in the mind
Swinging to the bottom of the nine
Obsession is the conversation I'm speaking
Come feed me more with that thing
Over and over again and again is the same thing
I keep on running back to you for that thing
Is that thing you give to me
that makes me go crazy
Makes me speak it in that language
Takes hold of me like a hostage
Feelings hit me hard like a hurricane
Full effect with lightning, thunder, wind and rain
Fill me up, wet me down, driving me insane
You are truly amazing, amazingly good
Always keep me in that kind of mood
I could not ask for a better satisfaction
Takes me to a higher dimension

25-12-2022

Thing Of Beauty

You are well Polish
without spots and blemish
You are greatly magnificent
This feeling felt so different
It can't be put into words
You play me on all chords
You look so good all I can do is admire
Like a butterfly glorious among flowers
You leave me fully astonish
Mouth open my statement I can't finish
You strike me like that
Beauty takes me like a heart attack
Yes I'm loving so much of it
That I became a victim of it
I'm falling for your beauty
Like the rising and falling of the waves of the sea
It takes me like the scent of a sweet incense
The impact of it is of great immense
I cannot turn away from you
My eyes are glued to you
I look at you with gladness
You are set in the right order
Portrait in Excellency like no other

24-5-2022

Me And Me Alone

My burdens are very heavy
you are not here with me
Stress and unhappiness got a hold of me
They are my newest company
You leave me and I'm all alone
All I have is my phone
Every night my soul weep
Bitterly until I fall asleep
Cannot deal with this thing
Haunted by these lonely feelings
My life is not good for I have lost my savior
God knows I need a fresh encounter
Worst state of my life I'm so miserable
Like a man can't put food on his table
Experience the depth of great heart
The pain and agony kill the heart
The brokenness of it is never sweet
cause my love is out of reach
What I've traded for it aint worth it
Now I'm losing ground hard to stop it
Hear me out you alone can please me
Any time I will take you back I'm always ready
Every day without you my life slowly drying up
Like the sun devouring a field of crops
Every time I cry my tears got bigger
My missing you gets harder and harder
Don't know what I'm gonna do
Missing those happy times with you
I have to deal with the facts
Really strike me, you ain't coming back

27-11-2022

My Words

Saw beauty let like a flame of fire
the sight of it makes me wonder
I drew near to look at you
I locked eyes steadfastly upon you
Stood speechlessly no words to say
You lighted up brighter than any sunny day
My eyes were filled with surprise
Never in my life have ever been that mesmerized
Wow! Beauty fills my eyes
To the greatest surprise
Lost to what's going on around me
Beauty blazes like a light from the heavenly
I'm overwhelmed by what I see
The flame of it engages me
I have seen, I have seen it all in you
All the host of heaven none looking like you
Put me in a different frame of mind
The qualities of you are so divine
From my spirit triggers within me
You shine in all of your glory
I can't get you out of the picture
Only one like you, there will never be another

26-11-2022

I Love Me Black Woman

For you are the foundation
I love you more than millions
you are the only one
With that kind of complexion
from when you born, you are a champion
me have to big up me black woman
You'd never leave me empty and dry
Give joy and peace you always satisfy
Have to turn you into a wifey
Protect you every day three hundred and sixty
you are a queen in a real life
Know how to make my life bright
You know how to keep me happy like you do
Not gonna put anything on anyone above you
Treat you with love and loyalty
With you I have life more abundantly
Gives me good food out of the kitchen
Always enjoy your loving delicious cooking
Your love is like life to the spirit
your vibes always keep it lit
Takes pride, taking care of your family
Your children proud to call you mummy
In my book, there is no leave
Forever with heart and soul, I cleave
You alone run in my thoughts

Like blood flowing to the heart
Your beauty grows from deep within
Everything you do, it keeps on shining
sweet substance comes from your nature
Can be seen, through your character
You are special and you are awesome
Faithful to the end, from day one
I love me black woman for your second to none
I love me black woman you are number one

1-12-2022

Prestigious

The way that you bloom
You are blessed from the womb
Love it when you shine like that
It's like praise on the altar
So glorious to see your brilliance
I cannot describe your appearance
It's so beautiful, out of this world
The sight of it brings to me endless joy
You shine, through pitch black darkness
It illuminates brighter than daylight
nothing can ever comprehend it
In every mouth that's the main topic
I could not see you with my natural two eyes
I have to look at you through the third eye
The spirit of your beauty will never die
The life of it, is beyond the sky
You are beautiful for now and tomorrow
Never drop off, always on another level
You saturate deep in my being
the joy of it is so enlightening

20-8-2022

Light up

You are totally pretty
Have more lines than Disney
Yes! You're pretty like that
You cannot be stopped
Beautiful, amazing to the Max
Over you dem get heart attack
Your looks get all the views
Leave Nuff at dem confuse
Your beauty is stock and pile
Ah you dem cannot style
You nar work off ah program
Only you alone are number one
don't need no makeup to look beautiful like that
you always ah lead, never follow the pack
No man can put you pon hold
You shine brighter than gold
Beauty is nothing without you
Calculator cannot calculate you
You can never be duplicated
Have it naturally cannot fake it
No one will ever be good as you
You made them take notes of you
You are truly a queen
Yes a goddess queen
In every way you ah dominate
You are the icing on the cake

25-6-2022

My Everyday Crush

Every time I desire to see you
I can't stop admiring you
Your beauty fills with light
It became my heart's delight
The way you shape captivates me
The sweetest beauty I ever see
What I've seen overcome me
It takes hold of me completely
Your flame burning beautifully through
Only one word could describe you beautiful
The way I stare at you
Expose my weakness for you
Feelings breaking me down, don't have a clue
Nothing cannot liberate me from you
All I can say is ello ello
As I fall below Ground Zero
I love the way that I'm feeling
It's definitely a good thing
So crazy to feel this way
I love it, I love it every single day
You're the flavor for the moment
In all that you do, I have to give you compliment
there's no space for nothing to intervene
For you're my coffee with the cream

2-9-2022

I'm Not Perfect

Done something in my life
I know that they are not nice
Over and over more than twice
In no way I cannot rejoice
Cause my conscience can't allow me to
Felt so bad for the things I do
I know that I'm not no Saint
In any way at all, I ain't
can't pretend for I'm not a hypocrite
Into that suit not going to fit
Because I am not righteous
Allow God to judge me first
Instead of throwing stones
I'm going to leave that alone

For I'm not perfect
but I'm working on it
To be honest not hiding it
This I have to admit
God knows I'm not perfect
Not going to pretend that I'm one
When I have so many flaws, I'm only human

The things I do I can't forget
Deep in my heart, I regret
don't wanna do bad things no more
Can't get back to that life I'm sure
How long I could keep it up
Real talk, God knows I'm fed up
Have to correct my mistakes
Praying every time I'm awake
Overcome in time with progress
I have to pass this test

29-10-2022

In A Moment

I see changes begin to happen
Hardship comes to an end
The darkness is shifted
My spirit has been uplifted
The tears I cried, they are no more
I'm walking through new doors
Light has shined for me to see
God turns everything around for me
Never again I have to fret
Now all of my needs are met
The ones that wish bad for me
I'm lifted up in the presence of my enemies
I have overcome the past
My life is in a different class
increased in wealth and endless blessings
After long years of so much suffering
Heaven comes to bless me
the riches of it flow endlessly
The freshness of it builds me up
Running over and over and non-stop
No more trying to figure things out
Living a life of laughter, without a doubt

29-10-2022

People

Dead conscience

Some people ah crazy news
Faster than a hurricane traveling 235mph
Only God alone can give me shelter
Not even an umbrella can save you
Their words are like wind
Blowing away everything
Going around Spread all the same come on-all lies there is
no truth in their words
They always had before you heard
You will just feed them, they Will kill you with their tongue
invade your life like the twin tower falling down
Not every kiss is a good kiss
Betrayal comes in a way of a kiss
not every greet is a true greeting
Snakes camouflage in a form of greeting
d me into the hands of my haters
To take my life for fuel to the fire
my blood not running in the midst of the land
like water poured from a cup in the hand
Sit around your table and break bread
And still, take bribes just to see you dead
Like brass, tin and iron gathered for the furnace
my life's not going to melt until it's finished
The wickedness of the wicked will catch up with you
If you think nobody sees you, God sees you.

8-10-2022

Fresh Up

The way you look pon me
Like me nah no body
Mi see yo facial expressions
It nah need no explanation
Me know yo nah wah me wah me
So don't feel sorry fu me
I'm not your typey, typey
I know you hurt me badly
But me nah go crazy, crazy
So stop cut style pon me
Me nah rich and bouggie
Me nah drive ah Bentley
Me poor and needy
Yo still nah better than me
When you say you don't want me
Can't explain how I feel
Wish that moment wasn't real
Send shock waves right through me
But I have to deal with reality
All I wanted was to be true to you
Love you just for you
When I thought I was winning
Now I have to think Again
Thought I was a blessing
Never knew I was a burden.

13-9-2022

Watch That

Like how you pop that
No one can watch that
Don't you trouble that so hot
Burns like fire under a pot
The way you shaking that thing
Damn! It's so mesmerizing
makes my heart sing
Oh! oh! What a feeling

This is So lit
you are killing it
getting all of my attention
I'm up in full emotion
This almost took me out
I had to shout it out
You leave me in a state of shock
from there hard for me to come back
Feelings I'm catching all
taking me like the federal

slowly you marinate my mind
I go out of control every time
you are doing is on a different level
The way how you do it
No one will ever come close to it
I go off in what I see
Got me saying Lord of mercy
looking at you this not normal
Wow! You are so phenomenal
You scratching like a bike tyre
With the smoke and the fire

20-11-2022

Smooth

Timeless Passionate

The way I look at you
Feelings I got almost cut me into two
never look at anyone this way
it's more than if I was short pay
What I'm feeling it's killing me
stronger than the flow of electricity
don't wanna lose now forget this feeling
the touch of it is overpowering
never get tired of it
takes me like an epidemic
and it's not fading away
feeling like this I don't get every day
it hits harder as it gets sweeter
as it grows it feels better and better
opens me up as it goes on
the impact takes me by storm
flows so hard, deep down until it reaches to its peak
races my heartbeat, drops down slow, so sweet
Can explain the feeling every time
like fire all through me even in the mind
feel like I'm hit, like an outbreak
there is no rest to it keeps me awake
this could never be outdated
years later I'm still enjoying it.

24-12-2022

Over Drive

Keep doing it, increase the pressure
Make me sweat, wanna feel the heat stronger
Burning me up with sweet pleasure
You need to increase the number
There is no slowing down or stopping
Drive faster, there's no stop light or pedestrian crossing
Do a hundred and fifty on one way
No traffic ahead, so take it away
Don't wanna see no trees
Just drive, sink your foot in the gas, please
Cause water to run off me like river
Until all of me, you take over
Don't take me home early wanna be late today
So you need to drive the long way
There is plenty of food on the table to eat
You cannot stop until you are complete
So you are very far from the end
That's just the introduction, you're not around the bend
No need for you to lose your head
Do it good so you will always eat bread
Hope your trucks full with water
Feelings blazing out of control like a forest fire
Don't drink water if you're not thirsty
You can't finish the work saying tired and weary
Play greedy and eat everything one time'
Next thing you making excuses for your crime
You gotta complete the job properly
So that you will be employed permanently.

5-12-2022

About The Author

My name is Gart Paulson DeShong, the first of five children, born under the sign of Gemini. I attended the Layou Government School followed by the Barrouallie Secondary School. I'm from St. Vincent and the Grenadines from the small town of Layou. I'm a police officer by profession. I enjoy playing sports and started writing at the tender age of 8 years old.

www.ingramcontent.com/pod-product-compliance
Lightning Source LLC
Chambersburg PA
CBHW070516220526
45467CB00002B/692